DATE			

BAKER & TAYLOR

Snowflakes, Sugar, and Salt

Crystals Up Close

by Chu Maki
photographs by Isamu Sekido

Lerner Publications Company • Minneapolis

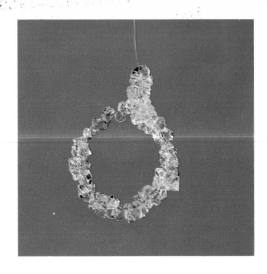

These are alum crystals. To learn how to make these crystals, turn to page 14.

These are alum crystals. To learn how to make these crystals, turn to page 14.

Series Editor: Susan Breckner Rose

This edition first published 1993
by Lerner Publications Company.
Originally published 1988 in Japanese under the title
Kesshou Zukuri by Kaisei-Sha Publishing Co., Ltd.

English translation rights arranged with Kaisei-Sha
Publishing Co., Ltd. through Japan Foreign-Rights Centre.

Library of Congress Cataloging-in-Publication Data

Maki, Chū, 1929-
    [Kesshō-zukuri. English]
    Snowflakes, sugar, and salt : crystals up close / by Chu Maki ;
photographs by Isamu Sekido.
        p.   cm.
    Translation of: Kesshō-zukuri.
    Summary: Examines, in text and illustrations, the characteristics
of various types of crystals found in everyday life.
    ISBN 0-8225-2903-3
    1. Crystals–Juvenile literature. [1. Crystals.] I. Sekido,
Isamu, 1946-   ill. II. Title.
QD906.3.M3513   1993
548–dc20   92-18538
                                                    CIP
                                                    AC

Manufactured in the United States of America

1 2 3 4 5 6 98 97 96 95 94 93

On a cold, cloudy day, snow falls from the sky. Up close, you see snowflakes clinging to the grasses. Do you know where snow comes from?

Snow is made high inside clouds. Clouds are made of tiny, invisible water droplets, called **water vapor.** High inside a cloud it is very cold, so the water vapor freezes into tiny bits of ice. The tiny bits of ice are called **ice crystals.** A single ice crystal is too small for you to see, even with a **microscope.**

Snow is made up of groups of many tiny ice crystals. **Crystals** have a fixed, orderly pattern and smooth, flat surfaces. Wind tosses around ice crystals in clouds, and when ice crystals bump into each other, they stick together in an orderly pattern. When many ice crystals stick together, they form a snowflake.

These snowflakes were photographed through a microscope, so they look much bigger than they really are. Because of the orderly pattern of ice crystals that make up snowflakes, snowflakes always have six sides. So far, no one has found snowflakes that look exactly alike.

When the air is dry, snowflakes look lacy, like the one on top. When the air is wetter, or more **humid,** snowflakes look more like solid plates of ice, like the ones on the bottom.

If you want to look at snowflakes up close, here's how you can catch the falling snow. Put a flat, dark, glass plate into the freezer. When the glass is very cold, bring it outside and catch a few falling snowflakes. Look at the crystal patterns of the flakes through a **magnifying glass.** Remember, the plate must be kept very cold or the snowflakes will melt.

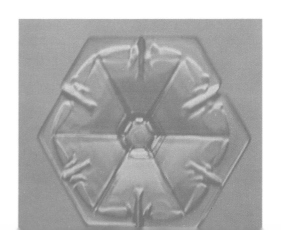

On a bitterly cold winter morning, ice frosts a window-pane. When the water vapor in the air of a heated room touches the cold glass of a window, the vapor freezes and forms into ice. Like snow, these ice patterns are formed from ice crystals.

Beautiful icicles hang down from the branches of a tree. Icicles are also formed from ice crystals. Icicles, as well as snow, the ice that forms on your windowpanes, and the ice cubes in your freezer, are all different **formations** of ice crystals.

Although ice crystals are too small for you to see, there are other kinds of crystals that you can see.

These crystals are used in cooking many foods, especially desserts. People love to eat these crystals. They taste sweet when you lick them. What are they?

These are sugar crystals, **magnified** 100 times!

SUGAR

FLOUR

ALUM

Sugar is not the only crystal formation you can find in the kitchen. Here are five different white powders that you can eat. Which ones are made up of crystals?

As you can see here, all five powders look pretty much alike. But if you look at them up close, you will see how different they really are.

SALT

BAKING SODA

The crystals that make up these powders are not as small as ice crystals. But they are small enough to be hard to see. To take a closer look at these powders, tape three magnifying glasses together. The powders look three times bigger than they would with just one magnifying glass.

SUGAR

FLOUR

ALUM

Now you can look at the powders and find out more about the shape of crystals. Remember, crystals form a regular, orderly pattern. Which powder is not made of crystals?

SALT

BAKING SODA

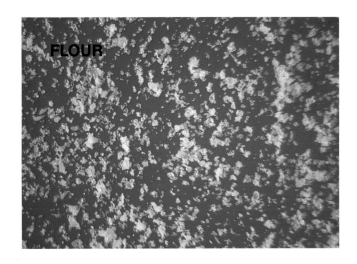

FLOUR

SUGAR

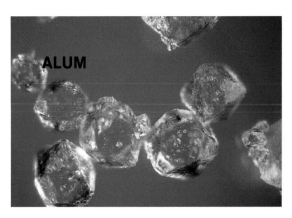

ALUM

SALT

BAKING SODA

On this page, the powders are magnified 50 times. The crystal shapes have sharp corners and flat sides. Only the flour looks different. Flour is not made of crystals. It comes from a wheat plant, which is a living thing. Only nonliving things are made up of crystals.

The shapes of alum and baking soda crystals depend upon how they were produced. But salt crystals are always shaped like dice. Even when they are crushed, salt crystals just break into smaller cubes.

You can make beautiful alum crystals, with the help of an adult. BE CAREFUL! Fire is dangerous. So always get an adult to help when you are using a burner or stove.

Things you need:
    granulated or powdered alum
    pot
    clear water glasses
    styrofoam box
    towel
    measuring spoons
    fishing line
    wire
    plastic wrap
    wooden chopsticks or pencils
    candy thermometer

Bend the wire into whatever shapes you like. Be sure that the shapes are small enough to hang inside your water glass. Here are some ideas for shapes.

Tie one end of a short piece of fishing line to each wire shape. Tie the other end to the middle of a chopstick or pencil. Lay the chopstick or pencil across the top of a glass so the wire shape is hanging inside the glass without touching the bottom.

Pour 2 cups of water into the pot. Add 11 tablespoons of alum to the water and stir. Heat the alum **solution** over a burner until the alum is **dissolved**. The solution will be about 150°F. When the alum is completely dissolved, remove the pot from the heat and let the alum solution start to cool.

Carefully pour the alum solution into the water glasses, just covering each wire shape. Cover the tops of the glasses with plastic wrap.

Once the temperature of the alum solution has cooled to about 120°F, **crystallization** begins. As the solution cools, the tiny alum crystals in the solution begin to move close to each other. When the alum crystals touch, they stick together in an orderly pattern.

When you see crystals sparkling in the alum solution, wrap the glasses in a towel and put them into a styrofoam box. Now wait for the glasses of alum solution to cool slowly.

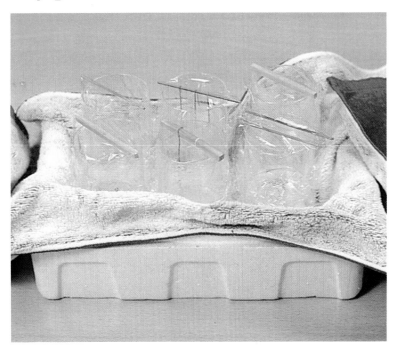

After one hour, carefully unwrap the towel from the glasses and look to see what is happening. If you let the alum solution cool for too long, the crystals sticking to the wire will get too large and fall off.

Remove the wire shapes when the crystals are about the same size as the crystals in the photos. Hang the wire shapes up to dry.

You can make earrings and pendants to give as presents to your friends. If you paint your crystals with varnish, they will last longer.

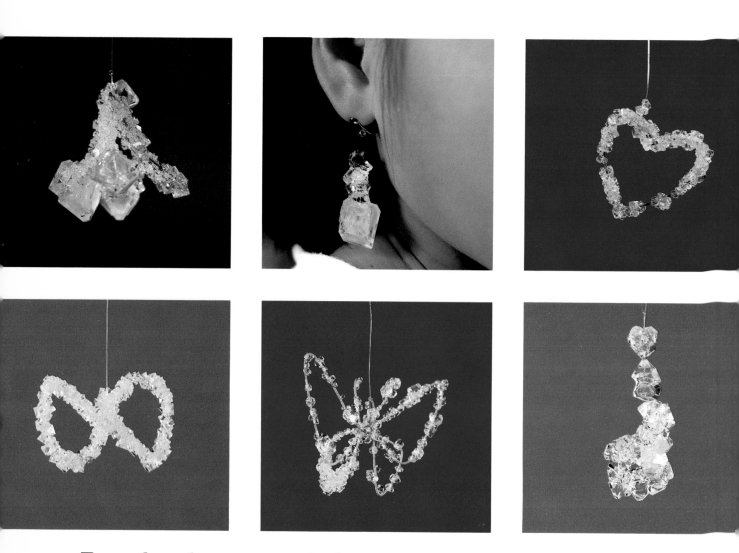

To make a large crystal, choose a crystal from the bottom of a glass to use as a "seed." Tie one end of a short piece of fishing line around the seed crystal. Tie the other end to the middle of a chopstick or pencil. Pour some alum solution into a glass. Lay the chopstick or pencil across the top of the glass so the seed crystal is hanging into the alum solution without touching the bottom.

20

Leave the seed crystal there to slowly form. If you first pour the alum solution through a coffee filter, the shape of the large crystal will be even more regular.

It will take about 24 hours for the large crystal to form. During this time, leave the glass in a towel-covered, styrofoam box, so that it will cool slowly. It is also important to keep the box perfectly still.

If you have ever been near the ocean, you can smell the salt in seawater. Salt is a crystal that is dissolved in seawater.

Crystals are dissolved in many different solutions in the natural world. Can you think of other crystals or solutions of crystals that are in the world around you?

GLOSSARY

crystal: a solid, nonliving object that has smooth, flat surfaces in an orderly, repeating form

crystallization: the making or forming of crystals

dissolve: to make or become liquid, as by melting in a liquid

formation: the way something is put together in a given shape or form

humid: air with a large amount of water vapor in it

ice crystals: tiny bits of ice

magnify: making an object look bigger

magnifying glass: a lens that, when you look through it, makes objects seem bigger

microscope: a tool that has many magnifying glasses in it and makes things look *much* bigger than they really are

solution: water with something dissolved in it

water vapor: tiny, invisible water droplets

24